LeBron James

SUPERSTARS IN THE WORLD OF BASKETBALL

LeBron James

Dwyane Wade

Kobe Bryant

Carmelo Anthony

Kevin Durant

Chris Paul

Dwight Howard

Rajon Rondo

Blake Griffin

Players & the Game Around the World

SUPERSTARS IN THE WORLD OF BASKETBALL

LeBron James

Shaina Indovino

Mason Crest

Mason Crest
450 Parkway Drive, Suite D
Broomall, PA 19008
www.masoncrest.com

Printed and bound in the United States of America.

First printing
9 8 7 6 5 4 3 2 1

Series ISBN: 978-1-4222-3101-2
ISBN: 978-1-4222-3109-8
ebook ISBN: 978-1-4222-8799-6

The Library of Congress has cataloged the
hardcopy format(s) as follows:
        Library of Congress Cataloging-in-Publication Data

Indovino, Shaina Carmel.
  Lebron James / Shaina Indovino.
    pages cm. — (Superstars in the world of basketball)
  ISBN 978-1-4222-3109-8 (hardback) — ISBN 978-1-4222-3101-2 (series) — ISBN 978-1-4222-8799-6 (ebook) 1. James, LeBron—Juvenile literature. 2. Basketball players—United States—Biography—Juvenile literature. I. Title.
  GV884.J36I54 2015
  796.323092—dc23
  [B]
                                    2014007853

Contents

1. Tough Beginnings 7

2. Training Hard 17

3. Breaking Records 27

4. LeBron James Today 37

Series Glossary of Key Terms 45

Find Out More 46

Index 47

About the Author & Picture Credits 48

KEY ICONS TO LOOK FOR:

Text-Dependent Questions: These questions send the reader back to the text for more careful attention to the evidence presented there.

Words to Understand: These words with their easy-to-understand definitions will increase the reader's understanding of the text, while building vocabulary skills.

Series Glossary of Key Terms: This back-of-the book glossary contains terminology used throughout this series. Words found here increase the reader's ability to read and comprehend higher-level books and articles in this field.

Research Projects: Readers are pointed toward areas of further inquiry connected to each chapter. Suggestions are provided for projects that encourage deeper research and analysis.

Sidebars: This boxed material within the main text allows readers to build knowledge, gain insights, explore possibilities, and broaden their perspectives by weaving together additional information to provide realistic and holistic perspectives.

Words to Understand

excelling: Doing very well or going beyond what people expect.

stability: When something has stability it doesn't change; it stays pretty much the same.

sacrifices: Giving up something so that something else that's better can exist.

Tough Beginnings

The year is 2013, and LeBron James is sweaty and exhausted as he looks up into the crowd. The auditorium is filled with his team's fans. They are clapping and cheering, because the Miami Heat just won its second NBA championship in a row. Throughout his basketball career, LeBron James has earned a lot of awards. He has competed for his home team and even for his country. As a member of the U.S. Olympic basketball team, he has won two Olympic gold medals. And in 2013, LeBron was named the Most Valuable Player (MVP) of the NBA finals.

LOOKING BACK

Being named MVP is nothing new to LeBron. In fact, this was his fourth time to receive the award. As he comes forward to make a speech, he is asked how he deals with the many pressures of competing. Professional athletes get asked this question all the time.

LeBron takes a moment to think before answering the question. Then he responds very

LeBron's started his life in Akron, Ohio, far from the beaches and lights of Miami. LeBron hasn't forgotten where he started, though. He may not play for an Ohio team, but LeBron's childhood made him into the man he is today.

plainly, "I can't worry what everybody says about me. I am LeBron James. From Akron, Ohio. From the inner city. I am not even supposed to be here." The crowd cheers before LeBron continues. "That's enough. Every night, I walk into the locker room; I see a number 6 with James on the back . . . I'm blessed."

When LeBron says he isn't supposed to be there, he is referring to how far he has come in life. Until he entered middle school, LeBron lived in some of the poorest neighborhoods of Akron. As a child from the inner city, the odds were against LeBron. Children from the inner city rarely have a lot of money growing up. Getting a good education isn't easy for these children. Finding a great basketball coach can be even harder.

Against all odds, LeBron rose to the occasion. He played basketball and was very good at it. Failure was not an option for LeBron. Even when life got hard, he kept trying. Today we know LeBron's hard work has paid off. His story shows us that you can become anything you set your mind to if you are dedicated enough. With a little help from his family and friends, LeBron became one of the most famous basketball players of all time. And he shows no signs of slowing down.

EARLY LIFE

LeBron Raymone James was born on December 30, 1984, in Akron, Ohio. His mother, Gloria James, was only sixteen years old. LeBron's father, Anthony McClelland, had no interest in raising his own child. He was an ex-convict and had spent a lot of time in prison. As a result, LeBron never met his father. This forced Gloria to raise LeBron alone. Her two brothers, Terry and Curt, helped out when they could.

Being a teenage mother and single parent made Gloria's life very difficult. She struggled to give LeBron the life she knew he deserved. It was hard for her to make enough money to support them both, because Gloria had a hard time finding a steady job. Gloria couldn't make enough money for her and LeBron to live on their own. So LeBron spent his first few years living with his mother in his grandmother's house.

When Gloria's mother died, Gloria couldn't pay the bills. The house they lived in was taken away by the city. A little while later, it was destroyed. Gloria and the young LeBron were forced to move around a lot after that. They stayed in apartments in some of the poorest neighborhoods in the city. LeBron and Gloria moved twelve times when he was between five and eight years old. The streets of the neighborhoods they lived in were often filled with crime and violence.

Even though life was hard for the young LeBron, Gloria did everything she could to shield him from the dangers of where they lived. His happiness and well-being were important to her.

When LeBron was just an infant, Gloria gave him a small hoop and ball to play with. He spent hours entertaining himself with these simple toys. Even at the age of three, LeBron showed promise. In an interview, his mother, Gloria, states, "I am not going to say I knew he was going to be a superstar, but you could tell he was fully determined. He wouldn't play with that toy set unless [the basketball hoop] was on the highest setting." LeBron's determination and need to challenge himself would follow him throughout his career.

At about the same time, Gloria began dating a man named Eddie Jackson. Like LeBron's biological father, Eddie was not a very good role model. Eddie spent a lot of time in jail as LeBron grew up. Even though Eddie was far from perfect, LeBron and Eddie formed a close bond.

By the time LeBron entered elementary school, he was *excelling* at sports. Two of his favorite sports were basketball and football. Michael Jordan was LeBron's favorite

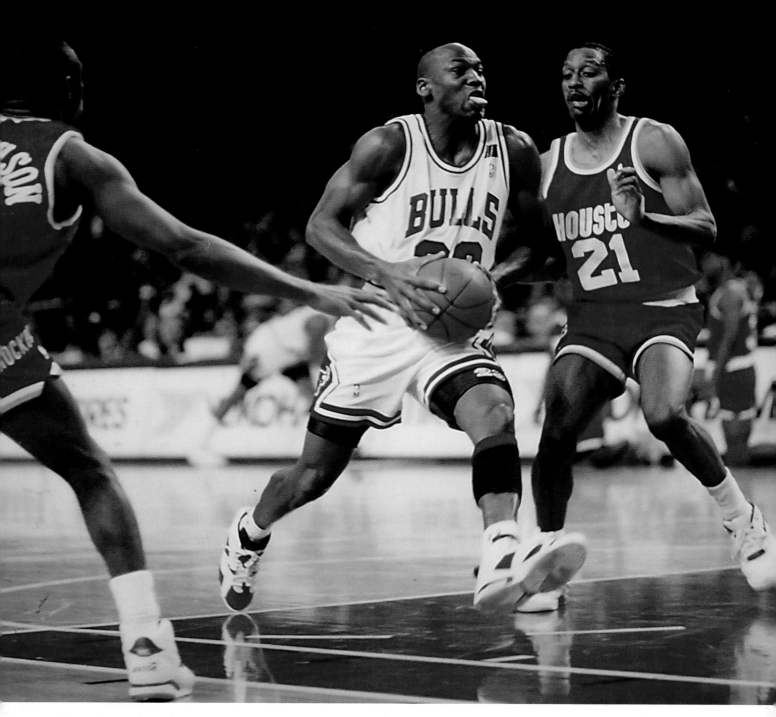

Few players have changed how people see the game of basketball more than Michael Jordan. For young players and fans growing up in the 1990s, Michael Jorden was a hero and a role model.

Make Connections

When LeBron started grade school, he realized just how different his life was from the other students. He was embarrassed by his home situation and tried to hide it from his classmates. He didn't want anyone to know just how much his family was struggling. Children who grow up without much money can have a hard time making and keeping friends. One reason is because they often move around a lot. Playing sports as a child was one of the ways LeBron coped with his difficult life.

basketball player. On the court, LeBron loved mimicking Jordan's moves. LeBron had difficulty making friends, but he didn't mind sharing the basketball with his teammates. He enjoyed watching everyone score and have a good time as they played together.

LeBron is still very thankful for how his mother helped him as he was growing up. In an interview with *WebMD*, LeBron said, "Whatever my mom could do or could not do, I also knew that nobody was more important in her life than I was." Gloria made sure LeBron stayed out of trouble. And she gave him the support he needed to achieve his dreams. "You have no idea of the security it gives you," LeBron continued. "How it makes you think, 'Man, I can get through this. I can survive.'"

MOVING IN WITH THE WALKERS

Most people know LeBron James as a famous basketball player. But when he was in elementary school, LeBron also enjoyed playing football. In his first year of peewee football,

Make Connections

It is no secret that most professional basketball players are very tall. The extra height helps them reach the basketball hoop and stop other players from scoring. LeBron is six feet, eight inches tall, so it might be surprising to know his mother is just five feet, five inches. But she has a lot of tall relatives. Thankfully, LeBron inherited his height from the rest of his family. In addition to being tall, basketball players must also be very agile and quick on their feet.

LeBron was already a good athlete when he was quite young. As a kid, LeBron learned about hard work and playing with a team in both basketball and football.

Research Project

Go online to find out more about Michael Jordan. To start, search for "Michael Jordan" using a search engine like Google or Bing. How many points did Michael score in his time in the NBA? Which teams did he play for? How many championships did Michael win? When did he leave basketball for good? Try to find an Air Jordan commercial on YouTube. Compare and contrast Michael and LeBron. How are their basketball careers similar? How are they different?

LeBron scored 19 touchdowns in 6 games. His coach, Frankie Walker, could already tell LeBron was something special. But little did he know LeBron would one day become a famous athlete!

Even though LeBron was doing well in sports, fourth grade was not a very good year for him. His grades suffered. He missed at least one hundred days of school and almost dropped out entirely. One reason he didn't go to school was because he had no way of getting there. It was hard for Gloria to find transportation.

Frankie Walker noticed LeBron wasn't going to school and was missing practice. He had a long talk with Gloria about LeBron's future. Eventually, Frankie offered to let LeBron live with him. He and his family could give LeBron a more stable life. Even though Gloria would miss LeBron, she knew it was for the best. "It was the hardest decision I'd made in my life," Gloria told *WebMD*. "But it was also one of the best. At that time in his life, he needed *stability*. It was hard, but I knew it was not about me. It was about him. I had to put him first." And Gloria's *sacrifices* would pay off.

Living with Frankie Walker was a big change from what LeBron was used to. In many ways, his life was less stressful. He didn't need to move around a lot and never worried about money. Frankie's family welcomed LeBron with open arms. "I loved being there. I loved being part of the flow that is a family," he wrote in the book *Shooting Stars*. LeBron was given chores and responsibilities, just like everyone else living there.

Even though LeBron's life changed a lot that year, his mother, Gloria, was never far away. He continued to see her on weekends.

Life began to look up for LeBron after he moved in with the Walkers. Unlike the year before, LeBron did not miss a day of school. It was also the year he started playing basketball on a real team. When Frankie saw how talented LeBron was, he invited him to join the Summit Lake Community Center Hornets. Frankie was the coach of the Hornets. LeBron played with them for a year, and his greatness started to show.

Sports were LeBron's passion growing up, but tough times at home sometimes made focusing on sports difficult for LeBron. Still, he kept working hard to be the best player that he could be. That hard work would soon get him a spot in the NBA.

Text-Dependent Questions

1. At the end of the 2013 Finals, how many times had LeBron been named MVP?

2. Why does LeBron say he isn't "supposed to be here?"

3. When LeBron's mother Gloria didn't have much money, what was their life like together?

4. Talk about Gloria's place in LeBron's life as a child. How did Gloria help LeBron become who he is today?

5. Why did Frankie Walker offer to let LeBron live with his family?

Gloria was eventually able to stand on her own two feet again. She rented an apartment large enough for her and LeBron. He moved in with his mother and continued to live with her for the most part until he graduated from high school. Whenever she had trouble finding the money to pay her rent, the Walkers temporarily took LeBron back in. It was important to the Walkers that LeBron had a place to stay whenever he needed one.

Words to Understand

professional: Having to do with something a person gets paid for doing as a job, rather than just a hobby or way to have fun.

potential: Having the ability to grow into something better in the future.

statistics: Numbers that show important information like points scored, assists made, and games won.

lottery: A way of picking an order for drafting players in which each team gets a ticket and then tickets are pulled randomly to decide which team will make the first draft pick.

TRAINING HARD

All athletes know that you do not become a **professional** overnight. Becoming the best takes a lot of hard work. You need to walk before you can run, and you need to crawl before you can walk.

JOINING A TRAVELING TEAM

By the time LeBron entered middle school, he already showed a lot of **potential**. He was tall, strong, and agile—three qualities that can make a great basketball player. His body alone wouldn't be enough to take him to the top, though. He needed to keep practicing to become even better.

As LeBron's skills improved, his family and friends continued to support him. He also met more coaches while playing for Frankie Walker. One of the most important was Dru Joyce II. Dru coached a basketball team known as the Shooting Stars. Unlike the Hornets, it was a traveling team. Traveling teams compete against other teams from all over the

By the time he was playing basketball for the Shooting Stars, LeBron could already dunk the ball. Basketball hoops are usually 10 feet off the ground, making LeBron's dunking even more amazing for his young age.

Make Connections

Since basketball is a team sport, it is not uncommon for some of the most talented players to rise together. Four members of the Shooting Stars became well known. Their names are LeBron James, Sian Cotton, Willie McGee, and Dru Joyce III. They made such a great team that they were known as the Fab Four. The Fab Four vowed never to split up and even chose to go to the same high school to stay together. Eventually, another great basketball player—Romeo Travis—joined them, and they became the Fab Five.

country. When LeBron was in the sixth grade, he was invited to play for the Shooting Stars. He continued playing with them through eighth grade.

LeBron met some of his closest friends while playing for the Shooting Stars. One of those friends was Dru Joyce III, his coach's son. Both LeBron and Dru played the position of point guard. LeBron, Dru, and their teammates practiced together whenever they could. They would gather at the Akron Jewish Community Center on Sunday nights, where Keith Dambrot, the former head basketball coach of Central Michigan University, coached them.

All the players on the Shooting Stars were very talented and dedicated to playing well. Together, they were able to make it to the Amateur Athletic Union nationals. The final games were held in Orlando, Florida. By now, LeBron was already well over six feet tall. He was even able to dunk the ball! The Shooting Stars played well in the finals, and it was a very close game. Unfortunately, they lost by just two points in the final game.

The Shooting Stars played together through Akron's St. Vincent-St. Mary High School. Unlike LeBron's previous schools, St. Vincent-St. Mary High School was a private school. Most of the students were very wealthy. LeBron and his teammates were not.

THE FIGHTING IRISH

LeBron started to get noticed as a basketball player in high school. In his freshman year, he became a member of the St. Vincent-St. Mary High School varsity team. They were known as the Fighting Irish. In his first year, LeBron averaged about 21 points per game. Thanks to LeBron and his teammates, the Fighting Irish were able to snag the Division III state title that year.

In his sophomore year, LeBron really began to shine. His average points per game increased to 25. His team finished with 26 wins and only 1 loss. LeBron and his teammates became state champions yet again. Out of every member of the Fighting Irish, LeBron attracted the most attention. He was named Ohio's Mr. Basketball and was selected to the

After growing up in Ohio, LeBron would soon be the star player of the Cleveland Cavaliers. He'd worked hard in high school to become the best player he could be and soon his hard work would pay off.

LeBron never went to college, where many future NBA players begin to get the league's attention. Instead, he entered the NBA draft after his final year in high school.

USA Today All-USA First Team. LeBron was the first sophomore to receive either of these awards.

LeBron's **statistics** continued to improve in his junior year. He averaged a total of 29 points per game that year. His rebounds per game also steadily increased. In his freshman year, he averaged 6 rebounds. By the time he reached his junior year, it had increased to 8. For a second year in a row, LeBron became Ohio's Mr. Basketball and a member of the *USA Today* All-USA First Team. He also became the first high school junior to be awarded the Gatorade National Player of the Year award. According to some reports, LeBron received his nickname, "King James," because of his achievements during his junior year.

During LeBron's junior year, he thought about trying to join the NBA. There was just one problem. The NBA did not accept anyone who had not completed high school. Because LeBron was still a junior, he was not eligible. He tried to get the NBA to change the rules, but it refused. LeBron needed to finish his high school education before he tried to play basketball professionally.

LeBron's senior year was even more exciting than his previous ones. His team had gained so much popularity that they began to play all over the country. His performance

The Cleveland Cavaliers play in the Quicken Loans Arena located in the heart of the city of Cleveland, Ohio. LeBron joining the Cavs was a big deal for many of the team's fans.

could be seen on many different television channels, including ESPN2. Like the previous years, he kept the title of Ohio's Mr. Basketball, and the Gatorade National Player of the Year. And he was on the *USA Today* All-USA First Team, again. He was also asked to play in several high school basketball all-star games. His final averages for his senior year were 31 points and almost 10 rebounds per game. By the end of his senior year, it was clear that he was ready to join the NBA.

THE NBA DRAFT

When LeBron turned eighteen, he was given a chance to show the professional basketball world what he was made of. Many NBA coaches had been watching him while he was in high school. They couldn't wait to bring him onto a professional team. When an athlete signs up for the NBA draft, he can be asked to join any national team.

So how does the NBA draft work? The NBA draft system might sound complicated. In reality, it is very simple. The draft system is designed to level the playing field for all NBA teams. For example, some teams are better than others. It wouldn't be fair to let the best team have the first pick of the athletes entering the draft. The best team would just keep getting better. And the worst team might get worse.

The NBA has found that the best way to make the game fair is to let the less-successful teams have first pick of new team members. The lowest-ranking teams in the NBA get to choose first, while the highest-ranking choose last. The order they pick is based on a drawing known as the draft *lottery*.

In 2003, the Cleveland Cavaliers won the draft lottery and made LeBron James their first pick. This couldn't have been a better situation for LeBron. Because Cleveland is in Ohio, LeBron didn't need to move very far. In fact, Cleveland is less than an hour away from his hometown of Akron.

LeBron considers himself lucky. Many rookie basketball players don't get to stay so close to home. They are forced to move wherever their team takes them. "My friends were excited that I was going to stay in Cleveland. It was real emotional for me and my family. I'm glad everything happened the way I wanted it to," LeBron said in an interview.

SALARIES AND ENDORSEMENTS

Some of the most successful athletes are millionaires. How do these athletes end up making so much money? There are two main ways. First, all athletes earn a salary from the team they play for. When a basketball player agrees to play for an NBA team, a contract is signed. That contract says how much money that basketball player will make each year. It also decides how long a basketball player will play for that team. How much money an NBA player makes depends on how popular and how successful he is. There may be financial bonuses based on playing statistics, increased attendance, and whether the team makes the championship series. A rookie usually makes a lot less money than a player who has been around awhile.

The second way an athlete makes money is through endorsements. When an athlete takes money to wear or use certain equipment, make advertisements, or speak on behalf of a person or company, he endorses that person or company. LeBron first endorsed Nike in 2003. Nike makes a lot of sports products but is best known for its line of shoes. After LeBron signed a contract with Nike, he only wore that company's sneakers. A line of sneakers was even released in his name.

When athletes do well, they make the products they endorse look good. If LeBron wears Nike shoes, fans might think the shoes help him run fast and score a lot on the court. If his fans believe Nike shoes are good, they might go out and buy them. Companies like Nike make a lot of money off endorsements because of the new customers they bring. The new customers figure that if a professional basketball player uses a certain shoe to compete in the NBA, then it must be good.

LeBron was drafted into the NBA and signed to Nike in the same year. This was a very big change from what he was used to. He had grown up without much money, and now

Text-Dependent Questions

1. Who were the Shooting Stars? What happened after LeBron joined the team?

2. Why couldn't LeBron join the NBA at first?

3. Why was LeBron happy to be drafted by the Cleveland Cavaliers?

4. Describe what an "endorsement" is. What endorsements has LeBron made?

he suddenly had millions of dollars. Many athletes in his situation might get carried away and buy a lot of expensive things, but LeBron was different. When asked if he did anything with his sudden wealth, he said, "I haven't done much. My friends probably spent more than I do. I don't need too much. Glamour and all that stuff don't excite me. I am just glad I have the game of basketball in my life."

Words to Understand

qualified: Officially recognized as being ready for a position or task.
nominated: Picked as a possible winner for an honor, award, or position.

BREAKING RECORDS

When LeBron started playing for the Cleveland Cavaliers, it marked a huge step in his career. He had worked very hard to become one of the best players in his high school. But when LeBron joined the NBA, he was just a rookie. Rookies are players who are new to the NBA. Usually, rookies do not do as well as more-experienced players. LeBron was now playing with the pros, and he needed to prove his skills as a basketball player all over again.

ROOKIE OF THE YEAR

LeBron wasted no time showing the world of basketball what he was made of. The year he joined the Cleveland Cavaliers, the team did very well. In his very first game, LeBron scored 25 points. Later in the season, he broke a record by scoring 41 points in a game

LeBron and Michael Jordan shared the number 23 when LeBron played with the Cavaliers. Later, LeBron would change his number to 6.

Basketball players are judged based on how well they perform different tasks. These statistics help the public know how strong each player is. They also help a coach decide which players to put on his or her team. There are five skill categories in basketball. The first, and most obvious, is the number of points scored. By scoring points, a basketball player helps his team win the game. The second is how many rebounds a player gets. When a player shoots to score but misses, anyone can grab the ball and continue playing. This is known as a rebound. The third category is assists. A player gets an assist if he helps make a basket but does not directly shoot the ball into the hoop. The final two categories are steals and blocked shots. In basketball, it is possible to steal the ball from another player or block a shot that is being made. Tall players like LeBron James have an easier time blocking shots than shorter players.

against the New Jersey Nets. At the age of nineteen, he became the youngest person in the NBA to ever score over 40 points in a single game.

Growing up, one of LeBron's idols was Michael Jordan. Today, Michael is still considered one of the best basketball players in history. In many ways, LeBron and Michael are very similar. From the moment Michael Jordan joined the NBA, he was a star. Like Michael Jordan before him, LeBron did very well in his rookie year. Before LeBron, there were only two players in history to average at least 20 points, 5 rebounds, and 5 assists per game in their first season. Michael Jordan was one of those players. In 2004 LeBron James became the third player in NBA history to do the same thing.

Because of his hard work, LeBron was named the Rookie of the Year in 2004. He became the first Cleveland Cavalier to receive this honor. Over the next few years, he led the Cavaliers to further victories and even to the NBA finals.

PROGRESS

Over the next four years, the Cleveland Cavaliers slowly improved, and so did LeBron. In the 2004–2005 season, he became the fifth person in history to average 27 points, 7 rebounds, and 7 assists per game. He also earned something known as a triple-double. To do this, he had to receive double digits in three of the five statistical categories. This is not easy to do! Very few basketball players ever manage to earn a triple-double. When LeBron earned his first triple-double, he scored 27 points, 11 rebounds, and 10 assists in a single game. His triple-doubles were well above his season averages.

In 2005 LeBron was asked to compete in the All-Star NBA Game. The NBA All-Star

Traveling to the playoffs with the Cavaliers was another step forward on LeBron's journey to become one of basketball's biggest stars. The team didn't win in 2006, but soon LeBron would be playing in more playoff games.

Make Connections

There are five positions on a basketball team. They are point guard, shooting guard, small forward, power forward, and center. Each position has an important role. Some positions are offensive, while others are defensive. A shooting guard, for example, is usually best at making long-range shots. Point guards are great at passing the ball to a player who is in a better position to score. Players who play center are usually very tall in order to reach the basket easily. Throughout LeBron's career, he has played several positions. Today, he most often plays as the small forward or power forward. Small and power forwards must shoot from up close and from far away. They also need to keep opponents from scoring. A person who plays these positions must be skilled in many areas. This is known as being versatile.

team consists of players from all over the United States. It is a great honor to be selected. Each year, fans and coaches vote on who they think would be the best players to compete. Two NBA All-Star teams are created based on where the players are from. One team is for the Eastern Conference and another is made up of teams from the Western Conference. Because Cleveland is located in Ohio, LeBron was part of the Eastern team.

LeBron was selected to join the NBA All-Star team for the second time in 2006. He led his team to victory in a very close match. The Eastern team scored 122 points, while the Western team scored 120 points. LeBron scored 29 of those 122 points. He was named the MVP of the NBA All-Star Game. And he was just 21 years old. This made him the youngest player in history to be named the game's MVP.

That same year, LeBron helped the Cleveland Cavaliers do something they hadn't done in almost ten years. With a 50–32 win/loss record, the Cleveland Cavaliers **qualified** for the playoffs. This was the first time since 1998. They did not win, but that didn't stop LeBron from doing well. He scored another triple-double in a playoff game against the Washington Wizards.

Over the next few years, the Cavaliers kept reaching the playoffs. LeBron also continued to be **nominated** for the NBA All-Star team. His skills kept improving, and so did his statistics. In one game in the Eastern Conference finals, LeBron scored a record 48 points. That year, the Cleveland Cavaliers reached the finals but lost to the San Antonio Spurs. LeBron's team went from not even making it into the playoffs to almost winning the championship in just a few short years.

By the 2007–2008 season, LeBron scoring a triple-double was not a rare sight. While other players struggle to get even one triple-double a season, LeBron earned seven.

LeBron (on the left) wears the Team USA uniform in a game against the Chinese basketball team during the 2008 Beijing Olympic Games.

Shortly after his twenty-third birthday, he broke another record. He had now racked up an impressive 10,000 points since joining the NBA. It wasn't long before he had scored more points than any NBA player in history.

THE OLYMPICS

Players in the NBA usually only compete against other players from U.S. teams. Some lucky NBA members are selected to be a part of the USA basketball team. This team competes in worldwide competitions. One such competition is the Olympics. Only a handful of the best basketball players in the United States will compete in the Olympic Games. The U.S. Olympic team usually does well.

As of 2013, LeBron has played in the Olympic Games three times. The first time was in 2004. During the 2004 Olympic Games, LeBron did not get to play very often. His coach decided to give more playing time to the more-experienced members on the U.S. team. It wasn't uncommon for LeBron to play fewer than fifteen minutes per game. LeBron was not happy about it. He was used to being a star. Learning how to sit on the bench while others played was hard for him. Despite LeBron not playing much, the U.S. team earned the bronze medal that year.

LeBron had learned his lesson by the next Olympics. He was willing to sit out while his teammates played. His coach decided to let LeBron play more in the 2008 Olympic Games after his attitude improved. When LeBron was allowed to play more, he was given a chance to truly shine. That year, the USA took home the gold by defeating Spain in the finals. Four years later, LeBron and the U.S. team defended the gold by beating the Spanish team again. LeBron's done amazing things playing in the Olympics for Team USA. But back at home, which team LeBron was playing for would become the biggest question in basketball.

In 2010, LeBron became a free agent. This meant he no longer had a contract with the Cavaliers. LeBron, like all free agents, was free to find a new team to play with. During this time, many teams tried to get him to sign onto their team. These teams wanted him for

LeBron leaps to dunk the ball during the 2008 Olympics in Beijing.

his talent and dedication to the sport of basketball. Just one week after becoming a free agent, LeBron made his choice. On July 8, 2010, LeBron announced his decision to join the Miami Heat. This began the next chapter in his national career.

Words to Understand

foundation: A nonprofit company or charity that works to achieve certain goals to make the world a better place.

LeBron James Today

LeBron's decision to join the Miami Heat was met with mixed feelings. LeBron played for the Cleveland Cavaliers from 2003 to 2010. During those seven seasons, he gained a lot of fans from Ohio. Many of those fans were disappointed to see him leave the Cavaliers to join another team. They believed LeBron should have remained loyal to the Cavaliers. After all, most of his success was gained by playing for that team for so long.

On the other hand, fans of the Miami Heat were very happy to gain LeBron as a team member. His skills would strengthen the team and help Miami win future championships. That year, two more talented free agents joined the Heat: Dwyane Wade and Chris Bosh. With two more strong players at his side, LeBron wouldn't feel pressured to do everything alone. When he played for the Cavaliers, he did most of the scoring. LeBron now hoped he could share the spotlight with the other two new players.

In any athlete's career, there is bound to be a time when he does not do so well. LeBron's first year with the Miami Heat was not very good. Learning to work with a new team can be a challenge. During the NBA finals that year, he did not score many points.

His average points per game dropped to just 17. The Heat lost the finals despite having three new talented players. Some people blamed LeBron for the loss. Losing the finals reminded LeBron that he can always improve.

In the 2011–2012 season, the world saw the LeBron from earlier years. His average score bounced back up to 27 points per game. He was named the MVP for a third time. LeBron truly proved what he was capable of in the 2012 playoffs. Whenever his team started to lose, LeBron pushed for more points. In some games, he scored over 40 points. Thanks to LeBron and the rest of the team, Miami became the champions that year. One year later, Miami defended its title. In 2013 the Miami Heat won the NBA championship for the second year in a row. LeBron was named MVP for the fourth time.

PERSONAL LIFE

Family has always been very important to LeBron. Without his mother, he wouldn't be where he is today. Now that he is a successful basketball star, LeBron needs all the support he can get. He has found that in a loving wife. At the age of sixteen, LeBron met his high school sweetheart. Her name is Savannah Brinson. They have been together ever since.

Although LeBron and Savannah both grew up in Akron, they were from different schools. Like LeBron, Savannah enjoyed sports. When they met, Savannah played softball and was a cheerleader. LeBron saw Savannah at a football game and invited her to one of his basketball games. She agreed to go, even though she didn't know how popular he was at his own school. When Savannah showed up to his basketball game, she was surprised. "I went, and I was like, 'Wow, this guy is pretty popular in here,'" she said in an interview with *Harper's Bazaar*.

Savannah and LeBron have stayed together through thick and thin. They have two sons. The eldest is named LeBron James Jr. He was born in 2004. Their youngest son, Bryce Maximus James, was born in 2007. After many years together, LeBron asked Savannah on New Year's Day to marry him. They married on September 14, 2013.

LeBron's moving to the Heat angered many Cleveland fans, but LeBron knew he had to move on to another team.

One of the reasons LeBron and Savannah have been together for so long is because of how well they get along. No matter what happens, they support each other. Athletes like LeBron need that support to stay strong on and off the court. "A person like myself always needs a great sidekick and a person you can rely on no matter the circumstances. And she's that," LeBron says. "She's got my back, and I love her for that."

At first, Savannah had a hard time getting used to the idea of living in Miami. But soon

LeBron greets fans in 2012. LeBron is one of the world's most famous basketball players today. Fans in Cleveland may not have liked his decision to play for Miami, but NBA fans still love LeBron.

LeBron has helped make the Miami Heat one of the most successful teams in the NBA, as well as one of the most popular.

after the family moved there, she changed her mind. Savannah loved the weather. The climate in Miami is very different from Cleveland. Ohio gets very cold in the winter. Snow can cover the ground for weeks. Miami, on the other hand, is usually pretty warm. It can rain, but it never snows. Many people from the northern states choose to go to Miami on vacation, because it stays warm all year. "When they told me it doesn't get any colder than 50 degrees, that sold me. We get below-zero weather in Cleveland," she says.

Today, LeBron and his wife own a mansion in Coconut Grove, which is one of the wealthiest neighborhoods in Miami. It cost LeBron millions of dollars to buy. Over the past few years, LeBron and his family gave gotten used to their new life in the Sunshine State. Yet as great as Miami is, they will never forget their pasts. Savannah still travels to Ohio frequently with her children while LeBron is training. "Cleveland is home. Nothing is going to change that," she says.

LeBron jumps to the basket past two other players. Today, LeBron has reached the top of the basketball world. Few other players can say they've reached the heights LeBron has. He's worked hard for the nickname "King James."

GIVING BACK

Basketball has always been an important part of LeBron's life. As a little kid, he played basketball to cope with the struggles of being poor. At the same time, LeBron understands just how important school is. He is thankful he stayed in school to finish his high school education. As a famous basketball player, he wants to help today's students follow in his footsteps.

LeBron has earned a lot of money throughout his career. He has said many times that money is not important to him. He enjoys the game for the joy it gives him and hopes others like it for the same reason. For LeBron, there are things more important than how much he makes. That is why he founded the LeBron James Family Foundation in 2004. Its aim is to help children get through school and live healthy lives. When LeBron started the *foundation*, he was just a teenager. Some of the money raised has gone toward the Akron Urban League and the Akron YMCA. In the past few years, the LeBron James Family Foundation has started building parks in inner cities.

Text-Dependent Questions

1. What was the reaction from Ohio fans when LeBron left the Cleveland Cavaliers for the Miami Heat? What did Miami fans think about LeBron joining their team?

2. Since LeBron joined the Miami Heat, how many championships has the team won? When did they win them?

3. Why was weather one part of LeBron's decision to join the Miami Heat?

4. Why is Savannah so important to LeBron? How long have they been together?

5. What is the goal of the LeBron James Family Foundation? Why did LeBron want to start the foundation?

Two years after starting his first foundation, LeBron began hosting the King's Academy Summer Basketball Camp. Any boy or girl from the age of seven to seventeen can attend. Like any other basketball camp, campers are taught basic basketball skills. What makes LeBron's camp different is that he wants to teach the campers so much more than that. "For me, the goal was to have a camp where kids could learn teamwork, learn to be unselfish on the court and off," James told *WebMD*. "Yes, we'll teach them to make a good jump shot, but they need to learn that the most important thing is school."

For LeBron, hosting the camp is not enough. He practices with the kids, too. When the campers are exercising, so is he. LeBron wants them to learn by example that even though basketball is hard work, it can also be very rewarding. "It's his mission to give back to the game that has given so much to him," says Damon Haley, the executive director of the camp.

With two NBA championship rings and many awards, LeBron James is on top of the basketball world. Many believe he is the best player in the NBA. Others say he may be the best player of all time. As fans debate just how good LeBron really is, he keeps proving his skill on the court. He's grown from a young man to a leader, from a boy who loved basketball to the game's biggest star. Today, LeBron has truly earned his nickname "King James." And he hopes to rule the game he loves for years to come.

Series Glossary of Key Terms

All-Star Game: A game where the best players in the league form two teams and play each other.

Assist: A pass that leads to scoring points. The player who passes the ball before the other scores a basket gets the assist.

Center: A player, normally the tallest on the team, who tries to score close to the basket and defend against the other team's offense using his size.

Championship: A set of games between the two top teams in the NBA to see who is the best.

Court: The wooden or concrete surface where basketball is played. In the NBA, courts are 94 feet by 50 feet.

Defensive: Working to keep the other team from scoring points.

Draft (noun): The way NBA teams pick players from college or high school teams.

Foul: A move against another player that is against the rules, mostly involving a player touching another in a way that is not fair play.

Jump shot: A shot made far from the basket (rather than under the basket) while the player is in the air.

Offensive: Working to score points against the other team.

Playoffs: Games at the end of the NBA season between the top teams in the league, ending in the Finals, in which the two top teams play each other.

Point guard: The player leading the team's offense, scoring points and setting up other players to score.

Power forward: A player who can both get in close to the basket and shoot from further away. On defense, power forwards defend against both close and far shots.

Rebound: Getting the ball back after a missed shot.

Rookie: A player in his first year in the NBA.

Scouts: People who search for new basketball players in high school or college who might one day play in the NBA.

Shooting guard: A player whose job is to take shots from far away from the basket. The shooting guard is usually the team's best long-range shooter.

Small forwards: Players whose main job is to score points close to the basket, working with the other players on the team's offense.

Steal: Take the ball from a player on the other team.

Tournament: A series of games between different teams in which the winning teams move on to play other winning teams and losing teams drop out of the competition.

Find Out More

ONLINE

ESPN.go.com: LeBron James Stats, News, Videos, Highlights, Pictures, Bio
espn.go.com/nba/player/_/id/1966/lebron-james

LeBron James on Facebook
www.facebook.com/LeBron

LeBron James on Twitter
www.twitter.com/KingJames

NBA.com: LeBron James Stats, Video, Bio, Profile
www.nba.com/playerfile/lebron_james

The Official Website of LeBron James
www.lebronjames.com

IN BOOKS

Mattern, Joanne. *LeBron James: Basketball Superstar (Sports Illustrated Kids: Superstar Athletes)*. Mankato, Minn.: Capstone, 2011.

Christopher, Matt and Stephanie Peters. *On the Court with . . . LeBron James: Basketball Superstar*. New York: Little, Brown Books for Young Readers, 2008.

Jacobs, L. R. *LeBron James: King of the Court (All Aboard Reading)*. New York: Grosset & Dunlap, 2009.

Christopher, Matt and Glenn Stout. *Michael Jordan: Legends in Sports*. New York: Little, Brown Books for Young Readers, 2008.

Index

Akron, Ohio 8–9, 19, 23, 38, 43
All-Star Game 31, 35

Brinson, Savannah 38

Cleveland Cavaliers 20, 22–23, 25, 27–31, 33, 37, 39, 44
Cleveland, Ohio 20, 22–25, 27, 29, 31, 33, 37, 39–41, 44

Dambrot, Keith 19

endorsements 24–25

football 9, 11–12, 23, 38

Hornets (rec team) 13, 17

Jackson, Eddie 9
James, Gloria 7–9, 11, 19, 21, 23, 29, 38, 42–44
Jordan, Michael 9–11, 13, 28–29, 35

Joyce II, Dru 17

LeBron James Family Foundation 43–44

McClelland, Anthony 9
Miami Heat 7, 35, 37–38, 43–44
middle school 8, 17
Most Valuable Player (MVP) 7, 15, 31, 35, 38

NBA draft 21, 23–24
NBA Finals 7, 29, 37
Nike 24–25
Olympic Games 32–33, 35

point guard 16, 19, 31

Shooting Stars (book) 13
Shooting Stars (team) 17–19, 25
St. Vincent-St. Mary High School 19

Walker, Frankie 13, 15, 17

About the Author

Shaina Indovino is a writer and illustrator living in Nesconset, New York. She graduated from Binghamton University, where she received degrees in sociology and English.

Picture Credits